MOUNTAIN CLIMBING

JIM HARGROVE

S. A. JOHNSON

Photographs by
JOHN YAWORSKY

Lerner Publications Company ▪ Minneapolis, Minnesota

ACKNOWLEDGMENTS: The photographs in this book have been provided by John Yaworsky with the exception of the following: pp. 15, 25, Cheryl Peterson; p. 38, Barbara McAdoo; p. 35, Swiss National Tourist Office; p. 43, Dick McGowan, Mountain Travel; p.46, S. A. Johnson. The authors wish to thank Randy Burns and Mike Dahlberg and the staff of Midwest Mountaineering for their help in the preparation of this book.

LIBRARY OF CONGRESS CATALOGING IN PUBLICATION DATA

Hargrove, Jim.
  Mountain climbing.

  (Superwheels & thrill sports)
  Summary: Explores mountaineering from the simplest rock climbs to more treacherous ascents, explaining techniques, equipment, special problems, and describing some famous climbs such as the Matterhorn, Annapurna, and Everest.
    1. Mountaineering—Juvenile literature. [1. Mountaineering] I. Johnson, Sylvia A. II. Title. III. Series.
GV200.H37   1983   796.5'22   82-21690
ISBN 0-8225-0505-3 (lib. bdg.)

Manufactured in the United States of America

International Standard Book Number: 0-8225-0505-3
Library of Congress Catalog Card Number: 82-21690

2 3 4 5 6 7 8 9 10 90 89 88 87 86 85 84

CONTENTS

INTRODUCTION

Most people are awed by the beauty of the world's mountains—the jagged peaks of Wyoming's Teton range, the snow-crusted European Alps, the lofty heights of the great Himalayas in Asia. The sight of a distant mountain range outlined against the sky inspires us with a sense of wonder at the powerful natural forces that created such an upheaval in the earth's surface.

For some people, mountains inspire not only wonder but also curiosity. These people want to explore the high places of the world and to understand the forces that have produced them. They want to climb to the top of the mountain peaks and to look down on the plains and rivers below. Such people are called mountaineers, and they are as much at home in the mountains as ordinary people are in their own backyards.

This book describes the sport of mountaineering and the skills that mountaineers use to climb to the tops of the highest peaks and to get back down again.

A peak in the Teton mountain range, Wyoming

3

Hiking or backpacking is a good way to get in shape for mountain climbing.

GETTING IN SHAPE

People do not become mountaineers by going out and climbing the first mountain that they see. Mountain climbing is a complicated sport that requires some very special skills and equipment. Most beginning mountaineers start out slowly, using only their own limbs and muscles and learning as their enthusiasm leads them to try bigger and bigger challenges.

Hiking in a hilly area is a good way to get in shape for mountain climbing and to learn some of the outdoor skills that you will need as a climber. One-day hikes or longer backpacking trips strengthen muscles and build endurance. Such expeditions also give hikers a chance to experience the beauty of mountain country, with its brilliant light and fresh, pine-scented air. Once you have been introduced to the pleasures of hiking in the hills, you will probably want to follow a trail that leads right up the mountain slope.

Much of the equipment needed for hikes and backpacking trips is part of a climber's gear as well. A pack containing a canteen of water, high-energy meals and snacks, a first-aid kit, maps, a compass, and rainwear is essential whether you are taking a one-day hike or a one-day climb. Camping equipment for longer climbs is similar to backpacking gear, except that it is extra lightweight and easy to carry. Clothes suitable for hiking are often practical for mountain climbing too. For both kinds of outdoor activities, you need layers of clothing that can be put on or taken off depending on the weather. Serious climbers usually wear special climbing boots, but sturdy hiking boots work well enough for beginners.

Hiking trips of several days require careful advance planning, and this kind of preparation is also needed in mountaineering. Checking maps of the area and choosing a route is important whether you are hiking in the hills or climbing up a mountainside. Keeping an eye on changes in the weather is another skill

Just like hikers and backpackers, mountaineers carry rain gear, extra sweaters, food, water, a map, and a compass in their packs. The shoes shown here are special rock climbing shoes with flexible soles.

that both climbers and backpackers must develop. It is not much fun to be caught in a storm while hiking, but heavy rain, wind, or snow in the mountains can be a source of real danger to climbers. People who spend a lot of time outdoors learn to respect the power of the elements and to prepare for sudden changes or extreme situations.

BEGINNING TO CLIMB

No matter where you are hiking, there will usually be a spot along the trail where you will pass a rocky hillside, an outcropping of rocks, or a jumble of large boulders. If you are like most hikers, the temptation to put down your pack and spend some time rock climbing is almost irresistible. Hikers who give in to that temptation have taken the first step toward becoming mountaineers.

Scrambling over boulders or up a rocky cliff may seem to be a rather ordinary outdoor pasttime, but it involves some of the very same skills used by the most experienced mountaineers. In all kinds of climbing, the basic requirement is finding footholds and handholds that will make it possible to move up a more-or-less vertical surface. Whether climbers are mounting a 10-foot-high cliff or the slope of a lofty mountain, they look for

No special equipment is needed to enjoy rock scrambling.

secure places in the rock surface where they can put their hands and feet. Spurs, knobs, ledges, and other projections make good handholds and stepping stones as a climber moves upward. Cracks and openings in the rock can also be used for the same purposes.

Experienced climbers have developed special ways of using the natural features of rocky surfaces in climbing. One such method is known as *jamming*, or forcing some part of the body into a crack or opening. Jams are usually used when the climber cannot find a projection or a horizontal opening as a resting place for hands or feet. In order to move upward, the climber must wedge fingers, a hand, or the toe of a boot into a vertical crack. In using a hand jam, the mountaineer often puts his or her hand into a crack and then makes a fist so the hand is held securely in the narrow opening. By using a combination of hand and foot jams, a climber can inch up a crack in an almost smooth rock wall.

Certain kinds of jamming methods make use of a climber's whole body. Many rock surfaces have vertical cracks or openings called *chimneys*, which are big enough for a person to get inside of. A narrow chimney can be climbed by pressing the back of the body against one rock wall and the feet against the opposite wall. By pushing with the feet and the palms of the hands, the climber can edge slowly upward. In a wider chimney, the climber may have to straddle the opening, with one hand and one foot on each side.

Whether climbers use special techniques like jamming or simply scramble up a cliffside,

This climber is using hand and foot jams to climb
a vertical crack in a rock wall.

they try to make their climb as safe as possible.
Before beginning the ascent, they study the
rock surface, looking for the easiest route up.
While climbing, they stop often to look ahead
and to locate the best places to put their
hands and feet. Good climbers try to move
only one limb at a time, leaving them with
three secure holds in case the new position
proves to be unsafe. They test each new hold
by shaking or kicking the rock before putting
their weight on it.

Despite all these precautions, climbers always
face the danger of falls and serious injury. In
order to make that danger as small as possible,
mountaineers make use of various kinds of
protective equipment. Learning how to use
such equipment is essential for anyone seriously
interested in mountain climbing.

These young climbers are practicing rope work. The proper use of the rope is the most important skill that a mountaineer must learn.

ON THE ROPES

Protection is the general term that describes the equipment and the methods that mountain climbers use to ensure their safety. The most important form of protection is the use of rope to connect one climber to another. A person climbing alone may be helpless if he or she starts to fall, but climbers roped together can help each other in a dangerous situation.

In most climbing expeditions, two or three people are roped together to form a climbing team. One person is chosen as the leader, and it is this climber who will decide on the route to be taken and who will begin the climb. After the leader has safely covered the first *pitch*, or section, of the route, the second climber follows and then the third. In this way, the members of the climbing team slowly and carefully make their way to the summit of the mountain.

The lifeline of the climbing team is the sturdy rope that joins them. Climbing rope is made out of nylon, and it is specially designed to stretch without breaking or losing its strength. Ropes come in lengths of 120, 150, or 165 feet (36, 45, or 49.5 meters). Each end of a length of rope is fastened to a member of the climbing team, either looped and knotted around the waist or tied to a special belt or harness made of nylon webbing. Extra rope is coiled and carried over a mountaineer's shoulder.

The ropes joining team members serve as a lifeline only when they are used properly. Careless or inexperienced handling of ropes may actually be a source of danger, causing one falling climber to pull down the other members of the team. People learning to climb spend weeks and months practicing the use of ropes. The basic skill they have to master is called *belaying*.

THE ART OF BELAYING

The general meaning of the word *belay* (beh-LAY) is "to secure or fasten a rope by attaching it to some immovable object." The first people to practice the art of belaying were sailors on the great sailing ships of the past. They raised or lowered the enormous canvas sails of their vessels by means of ropes that were secured by twisting them around cleats or pegs. Modern sailors still belay ropes in the old way, but mountaineers have developed belaying into a new and complicated art.

When climbers belay a rope, the immovable object that they attach it to is the mountain itself. Rock surfaces don't come equipped with cleats or pegs, but mountaineers have invented various pieces of equipment that make it easier to secure the rope to the rock. The second essential element in belaying is the *belayer*, the person who controls the rope,

letting it out and pulling it in according to the needs of the climber.

Let's take a look at a typical climbing situation to see how belaying actually works. A team of two climbers is ready to begin the ascent of a mountain slope. The leader is an experienced mountaineer, a woman who has been climbing for 10 years. Her companion is a younger woman who has learned the basic climbing skills but has not had very much actual experience.

With the climbing rope securely fastened to both women, the leader starts up the first pitch. The pitch is steep but not particularly difficult for an experienced climber, and the leader reaches her goal quickly. Then, seating herself on a ledge of rock, she prepares to act as belayer for the second climber, who will need protection for the climb. To set up the belay, the leader takes a *sling*, a loop of strong nylon webbing, from among the pieces

Mountaineers use nylon slings (center) and metal clips called carabiners (right) in setting up belays and for many other purposes.

of equipment hanging from her climbing belt. She loops the sling over a projection of rock behind her and attaches it to the back of her belt with a *carabiner* (kar-uh-BEE-nuhr), an oval-shaped metal clip. Now her body is firmly anchored to the mountain, and she will be able to support the second climber in case of a fall.

The climbing rope, one end of which is still attached to each climber's waist, must be handled in a special way during a belay. The belayer loops her part of the rope around her body at hip level. Then she grips the rope on either side with her hands. One hand holds the section of rope that extends to the second climber waiting below. During the belay, this hand will be used to pull in the rope as the climber mounts. The other hand grips the rope after it has passed around the belayer's body. This is the *braking hand*; if the second climber falls, the belayer will clamp down hard with this hand, at the same time pulling the rope forward against her body. The combination of this strong grip, plus the friction created by the rope passing around the belayer's body, will be able to stop the fall and save the climber from serious injury.

Instead of passing the rope around her body, the leader might use a mechanical device to control the rope and to stop a fall. One such device is a *belay plate*, shown in the pictures on the opposite page. A loop of the rope is passed through the opening in the metal plate and clipped into a carabiner that is fastened to the front of the belayer's belt.

As the second climber mounts, the belayer pulls the rope through the plate just as she would pull it around her body. If the climber falls, the belayer will use her braking hand to pull the rope hard in the direction opposite to the fall. This action will push the belay plate back against the carabiner, and the resulting friction will stop the movement of the rope.

When the leader has finished setting up the belay, she calls down to the second climber, "Belay on." The younger woman calls back, "Climbing," and she begins to pick her way slowly up the pitch. If the two climbers could not hear each other, for instance, because of a strong wind, they would communicate by jerking the rope in a prearranged code.

As the second climber mounts, she does not hold onto the rope or use it in any way to assist her climb. The rope is there only for protection, and she must depend on her climbing skills to reach her goal. Moving with care and precision, the young climber finally reaches the ledge where the leader is waiting. The team members sit and rest while discussing the next stage of the climb. Then the leader unfastens the belaying anchor and starts up the second pitch.

Left: A belayer using a belay plate. In this photograph, the belayer's right hand is his braking hand. *Right*: These two photographs show how the climbing rope passes through the opening in the belay plate and through the carabiner behind it.

This large chock would be used as an anchor in a wide crack.

The belay described here is the simplest and easiest kind, with the belayer positioned above the climber and firmly attached to a natural anchor. In more difficult belays, there is no convenient spur of rock to serve as an anchor, and the belayer must use special equipment to attach himself or herself to the rock. The most commonly used device in setting up an artificial anchor is a *chock* or *nut*, a chunky piece of metal that looks something like an ordinary nut used to secure a screw or bolt.

Mountaineers carry chocks of various sizes with them on a climb. When a belaying anchor is needed, a climber selects a chock and forces it down into a crack in the rock so that it is firmly wedged in the narrowest part. Chocks have loops of wire or webbing threaded through them that can be attached to a climber's belt by means of slings and carabiners. Attached to a properly placed chock, a belayer is anchored securely and ready to stop another climber's fall.

Belaying becomes particularly complicated and difficult when the belayer is positioned below the climber needing protection. This situation exists when the leader of a climb must be belayed by other team members. In many climbs, the leader needs protection on some or all of the pitches. Belaying the leader requires some very special techniques.

The most important requirement in this kind of belay is making sure that the distance the leader might fall is as short as possible. Without any special protection, a leader belayed from below would fall the distance between his or her position and that of the belayer's, plus that same distance below the point where the belayer is anchored. For instance, a leader 25 feet above the belayer would fall a total of at least 50 feet before the climbing rope could stop the fall. A fall of this length could be extremely dangerous. In order to shorten the distance the leader might fall, climbers use a technique called a *running belay*.

A running belay is based on the same principle of protection as other belays; the leader is connected by rope to another climber who is anchored to the rock and ready to stop a fall. What is special about this kind of belay is what happens to the rope between the two climbers. As the leader moves up the pitch, he or she places a chock in the rock and attaches the climbing rope to it with a carabiner. The rope runs freely through the opening in the metal clip so that the leader can continue to climb.

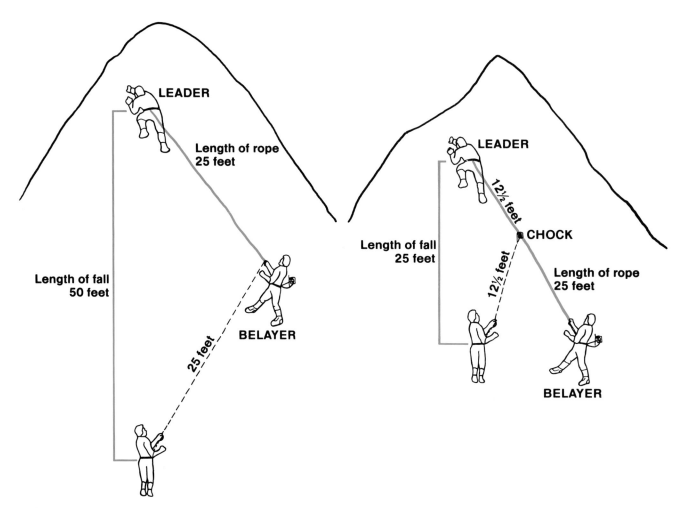

These drawings show how the use of a running belay shortens the distance that the leader of a climbing team might fall. In the drawing on the left, the leader would fall a total of 50 feet before the belayer could stop the fall. Protected by a running belay, the leader on the right would fall only 25 feet—twice the distance between the leader's position and the chock.

Positioned on a ledge below, the belayer slowly feeds out the rope as the team leader moves upward. As usual, the belayer is prepared to clamp down hard on the rope in case of a fall. If the leader does fall, the length of the fall will be twice the distance between his or her position and the chock, not between the leader and the belayer. By putting in a series of chocks while climbing a difficult pitch, the leader can make sure that a fall at any one time will be short enough not to be excessively dangerous.

The belayer in a running belay has to take special precautions to make sure that he or she can control the leader's fall. Since the leader is above the belayer, the pull on the rope would come from above, not from below as in the simple belay described earlier. If the belayer is not anchored properly, he or she could be knocked over by a sudden upward jerk on the rope. Even more dangerous, the belaying anchor could be pulled up and off a vertical spur of rock, losing the whole belay. The anchor in a running belay must be chosen so that it can withstand the upward pull on the rope caused by the leader's fall. Often a belayer will use two separate anchors, one for the upward movement, the other designed to hold in case a fall takes the leader below the point where the belayer is anchored.

Only the leader of a climbing team needs to be protected by a running belay. Once the leader reaches the top of a pitch, he or she can belay the other team members from above. The next climber up the pitch removes the chocks and carabiners used for the running belay. These pieces of climbing equipment are expensive, and mountaineers don't want to lose them. Even more important, they don't want to leave discarded equipment behind to spoil the natural surface of the rock.

Left: The leader of a climbing team protected by a running belay. *Above:* The rope in a running belay passes through a carabiner attached to the mountain slope by a chock and a sling.

COMING DOWN FAST

Climbing up a mountain is hard, demanding work, requiring skill, care, and endurance. It is also exciting and satisfying, as climbers overcome the special problems of each pitch and move closer and closer to their goal. When a climbing team finally reaches the mountain peak, its members are tired but happy. They shake hands, congratulating each other on their achievement. Photographs are taken, and a few quiet moments are spent enjoying the magnificent view. Then it is time to descend.

In many climbs, going down the mountain is just like coming up, only the directions are reversed. Belaying each other from above and below, the climbers move carefully down each pitch, searching for safe holds in the rock. Sometimes, however, mountaineers find

A climber on top of Half Dome, a mountain in California's beautiful Yosemite Valley

it necessary to come down fast. If weather conditions are threatening or if night is fast approaching, a slow descent on a steep slope could be extremely dangerous. In this kind of situation, climbers might use the technique of *rappeling* (rah-PELL-ing) to get down the mountain.

When a climber rappels, he or she slides down a rope that is anchored at the top of a pitch. Anchors for rappels are basically the same as those used for belays—slings firmly attached to chocks or projections of rock. The anchoring equipment can be used only once by a climbing team. There is no way to go back and pick it up after the last climber has rappeled down, so it has to be left behind on the mountain slope.

The rope used in a rappel can be pulled down and used again. This is because the rope is doubled by passing it through the anchor sling so that both halves dangle down the pitch. After the last climber has descended, one end of the rope is pulled, bringing the whole thing down.

Exactly how does a climber slide down a rappel rope? In the simplest kind of rappel, the rope is first wrapped around the body. To set up the rappel, the climber stands facing the anchor and passes the doubled rope between the legs and behind one thigh. The rope is then brought across the chest diagonally and over the opposite shoulder so that its free ends hang down the climber's back. The climber uses one hand to hold the rope as it comes from the anchor. The other hand grips the rope after it has passed around the body; this is the braking hand, used to control the speed of the rappel and to stop it if necessary.

With the rappeling rope in place, the climber

A group of climbers learning the technique of rappeling

simply starts backing down the mountain slope. The rope slides around his or her body, creating a friction that makes the descent slow and controlled. During a rappel, the climber is in a sitting position, leaning away from the slope with feet against the rock surface. As a slope becomes steeper, the rappeler's body will become almost horizontal. At points where the slope curves inward, the rappeler will not touch the rock at all but will be supported only by the rope.

This basic rappel uses simple equipment and is not difficult to learn. It does have one big drawback, however. The climber's body is subjected to the friction of the moving rope, which can be painful or even cause rope burns. Because of this problem, mountaineers have developed more complicated methods of rappeling in which the rope is not wrapped around the body. Most of these methods use harnesses to which carabiners or special metal rings are attached. The rappeling rope passes through the pieces of hardware, which absorb most of the friction. With this kind of equipment, rappelers can avoid the discomfort and possible injury caused by the moving rope.

No matter what kind of equipment is used, many mountaineers consider rappeling a fairly risky technique to be used only with great caution. Rappels are usually made on very steep slopes where a fall could be fatal. Because of this special danger, rappelers are often belayed by other members of the climbing team. A rappel can be an exciting and dramatic technique, but for most mountaineers, the real test of climbing skill is not sliding down a rope but moving inch by cautious inch over the rock surface of a difficult pitch.

This climber is rappeling down a mountain slope. Instead of wrapping the doubled rope around his body, he has passed it through several sets of carabiners that are attached to his climbing harness (above). As he descends, the rope slides smoothly through the carabiners. The rappeler is using his left hand as a brake to control the speed of his descent.

Mountaineers in the Sierra Nevada mountain range of California often face the challenge of climbing on ice and snow.

THE CHALLENGE OF ICE AND SNOW

Some mountaineers limit their climbing to rocky cliffs and peaks, but others find the most satisfaction in scaling snow-covered slopes and walls of sheer ice. Snow and ice climbing is a very important part of mountaineering. The highest mountain peaks in the world are always snow-covered, and even lower mountains have patches of snow and ice on them during most of the year. Anyone who is seriously interested in climbing usually reaches a point where he or she is ready to face the challenge of snow and ice.

Mountaineers climbing on snow and ice have the same goal as rock climbers—they want to get to the top of the pitch or the peak in the easiest and safest way. The techniques used for snow and ice climbing are different, however, because the climbing surface is so different. Snow and ice are generally much smoother and more slippery than rock. Getting a foothold on a slope of crusty snow or slick ice requires different methods and pieces of equipment than climbing up a craggy mountainside. Protection on ice and snow also has very special requirements.

Mountaineers have developed various methods of making their way over snow and ice. The simplest way is using the feet to kick or stamp out steps in a snow-covered slope. This works well when the snow is fairly soft yet firm enough to hold the climber's weight. On hard snow or on ice, kicking doesn't work, but it is possible to cut steps in the surface. For this job, mountaineers use an *ice ax*, an essential tool for snow and ice climbing. An ice ax has a pointed shaft and a head with a sharp pick on one end and a broader blade on the other end. A climber uses the pick end to chop out small footholds in the ice or snow. Many of the great climbs of the past, especially those in the European Alps, were done by climbers who vigorously and skillfully chopped their way up long, ice-covered mountain slopes.

Today the ice ax is still an important piece of mountaineering equipment, but many climbers prefer to use *crampons* (KRAM-pahns) when they tackle hard snow and ice. A crampon is a metal frame with sharp spikes on its lower surface. Strapped to climbing boots, crampons give mountaineers a firm foothold on the most slippery surfaces. In ascending a moderate slope, a climber puts the bottoms of the crampons flat against the surface so that the spikes bite into the ice or snow. Climbing a steep slope might require the use of special crampons with two extra spikes sticking out at the front. The front spikes alone are jabbed into the hard surface, creating small toeholds. Handholds can be formed by sticking the pick of the ice ax into the ice and holding onto the handle. Using this climbing technique, mountaineers can work their way up nearly vertical walls of ice.

When climbing on slippery ice or snow, good protection is vital. Belaying is the standard form of protection in this kind of climb, but it cannot always be done by the usual methods. If possible, ice and snow climbers try to anchor their belays in outcroppings of rock or in boulders frozen into the ice. An anchor attached to rock is dependable, but it is also possible to place secure belay anchors directly into snow or ice.

Using an ice ax and crampons, a mountaineer makes her way up a steep slope.

When anchoring in snow, climbers often use a *snow fluke*, a metal plate with a cable attached to it. A fluke is buried deep in the snow at an angle to the slope, with the cable extending above the surface and connected to the belayer. If a belayed climber falls, the snow in front of the fluke will support the fall. Many snow flukes are specially designed so that they are driven deeper into the snow by the force exerted on the connecting cable.

Belay anchors on ice are made with different pieces of hardware. Long *ice screws* with eyes in one end can be twisted into hard ice and used as anchoring points for belaying slings. *Pitons* (PEE-tahns), thin metal blades with rings or eyes attached, have to be driven into the surface with ice hammers. Both screws and pitons make it possible for a belayer to be firmly anchored to the ice and ready to

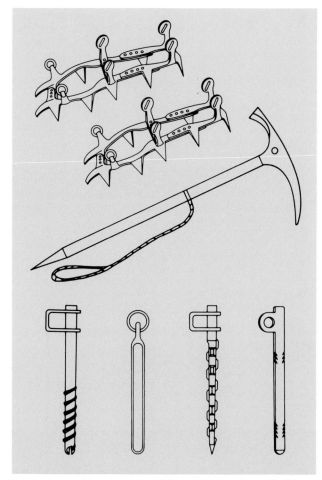

Some essential equipment for snow and ice climbing: crampons (top); an ice ax (center); ice screws and pitons (bottom).

protect a fellow climber.

Although protection in snow and ice climbing presents special kinds of problems, it also has one special advantage. Individual climbers can protect themselves from falling more easily on snow and ice than on rock. When rock climbers slip, the rope is their only defense against a serious fall. A climber on snow or soft ice can also use the technique of *self-arrest* to stop a fall. If a climber slips and begins sliding down a snow-covered slope, he or she can quickly dig the pick of the ice ax into the snow and halt the fall. Mountaineers spend hours practicing self-arrest techniques so that they can get the pick into the snow immediately no matter what position they are in when they start to fall. Such training has saved many climbers from a long and dangerous slide down a slippery slope.

The technique of self-arrest makes it possible for an individual climber to stop a fall on a snowy slope.

Meeting the challenge of ice and snow requires learning many special climbing techniques. It also forces climbers to be particularly aware of the natural hazards they may meet. Under changing weather conditions, surfaces of snow or ice may suddenly crumble underfoot or become too soft to hold an anchor. At certain times of year, avalanches made up of tons of loose snow and ice may come roaring down the mountainside, sweeping away everything in their path. Dangerous crevasses (kreh-VASSES), deep cracks in the ice of glaciers, may be hidden under a thin cover of snow.

Mountaineers must be prepared to face these hazards and to deal with them sensibly and safely. Perhaps the greatest natural danger they will meet is the cold and changeable weather of the high mountains. Clothing and equipment must be planned to ensure survival under extreme weather conditions. Snow and ice climbers usually take emergency supplies with them in case they are forced to stay on the mountain slopes longer than scheduled. They know that cold, lack of food or water, and exhaustion can be their biggest enemies in the dangerous but beautiful world of the high mountains.

For many mountaineers, that lofty, snow-covered world is the goal of their climbing careers. They want to test their skills and endurance against the challenge of the very highest peaks. Some of those peaks have been conquered already by climbers whose accomplishments provide inspiration for newcomers to the world of climbing. Here are the stories of a few of those great mountaineers and their achievements.

With their equipment piled around them, these climbers are waiting out a storm on Mount Shasta in California's Cascade Range.

EARLY CLIMBERS IN THE ALPS

Mountain climbing first developed as a sport in the Alps, a beautiful system of mountains located in south-central Europe. In the 1800s, the steep slopes and snow-covered peaks of the Alps attracted people from all over the world who were fascinated by the challenge of mountaineering. The peaks of the Alps offered plenty of challenge, but they also held some advantages for beginning climbers. Alpine mountains are not extremely high—all peaks are under 16,000 feet (4,800 meters)—and they can usually be climbed in one or two days. For these short climbs, early mountaineers needed a minimum of camping gear and provisions. Today, the word *Alpine* is used to describe any short-term climb of this kind, no matter where the climb takes place.

One of the earliest and most famous Alpine climbs that took place in the Alps themselves was the ascent of the Matterhorn in 1865. Located in the part of the Alps between Italy and Switzerland, the Matterhorn is a beautiful, steep-sided peak whose upper slopes are always covered with snow. During the early 1800s, many climbers had tried but failed to reach the 14,692-foot (4,478-meter) summit of the Matterhorn. Then in 1865, three separate parties of British mountaineers, led by Edward Whymper, Lord Francis Douglas, and Reverend

The snowy peak of the Matterhorn rises above the houses of a village in the Swiss Alps.

Charles Hudson, joined forces for another attempt at the peak. Whymper had tried to climb the Matterhorn seven times before, always from the Italian side. His repeated failures convinced the group to try the Swiss side instead.

The climb began well. By noon on the first day, the party reached the spot where they had planned to set up camp. On the following day, Whymper and one other member of the team made the ascent to the top of the Matterhorn with little trouble.

It was on the way down the mountain that things began to go wrong. For the descent, the climbers roped themselves together. No one knows why, but they used their poorest rope, which was frayed and weak.

One of the climbers, Douglas Hadow, was quite inexperienced. He had tried to pass himself off as a skilled mountaineer, but during the ascent, the others had been required to assist him many times. Soon after the group began climbing down, Hadow slipped and fell. He crashed into the climber below him. Higher up the mountain, Whymper and the other climbers felt a sudden jerk on the rope. They clung to the mountain and momentarily managed to stop their friends from falling. Then the rope snapped, and four members of the team tumbled more than 4,000 feet (almost 1,200 meters) to their deaths.

The Matterhorn had been conquered, but a price had been paid in human lives. It would not be the last time that mountaineers would risk injury and death to reach the summit of an awesome mountain.

ON THE ROOF OF THE WORLD: CLIMBING THE HIMALAYAS

After 1865, many mountaineers succeeded in climbing the Matterhorn and the other high peaks of the Alps. But it was not until almost 100 years later that climbers faced the challenge of the highest mountains in the world, the great Himalayas. Located in southern Asia, the Himalayan system includes the 14 giants that mountaineers call the "8,000-meter peaks." All towering over 8,000 meters (26,400 feet), these mountains are considered the supreme test of a mountaineer's courage and ability.

Climbing in the Himalayas has always been a special kind of challenge because of the severe conditions that mountaineers face. Just reaching the remote area north of India where the mountains are located requires days of travel, often on foot, through dense tropical forests and across torrential rivers. Large expeditions made up of many people are required to transport all the supplies that mountaineers need for the long and difficult Himalayan climbs. Most expeditions enlist the aid of local porters and guides called Sherpas, who are familiar with the rugged territory and used to the severe climate of the mountains.

Unlike Alpine climbing, climbing a Himalayan peak cannot be done in one or two days. An attempt to reach the summit may take many days or even weeks. Climbers start out from a large base camp set up on the lower slopes of the mountain. As they move up the mountain, they establish a series of smaller camps where they spend the night, resting and sheltering against the bitter cold. Only a

The lofty, snow-covered Himalayas offer a challenge to climbers all over the world.

few members of the climbing team make the final assault on the peak, and they may take nothing more than a tiny tent and a small supply of food with them as they struggle up the icy, wind-swept slopes to the summit of the mountain.

The hardships and danger of Himalayan climbing are well illustrated by the dramatic story of the conquest of the lofty mountain known as Annapurna. Located in the small Asian country of Nepal, Annapurna was the first of the 8,000-meter peaks to be climbed. In 1950, a Frenchman, Maurice Herzog, led a huge climbing expedition to Nepal, ready to tackle the giant mountain. After weeks spent hiking to the base of Annapurna and then studying the mountain to find the best route to the top, Herzog and his group started to climb. They established six small camps on the icy slopes of the mountain in addition to the large base camp where supplies were stored.

As the climbers moved higher and higher, they suffered from lack of oxygen caused by the high altitude. Difficulty in breathing and bitter cold weakened them, and they often had to move back down to lower camps to recover their strength before continuing the climb. After days of strenuous effort, often struggling through waist-deep snow, Herzog and one other climber had almost made it to the summit. They spent the night of June 2, 1950, in the small tent they called Camp Five, set up on a narrow shelf of snow cut into a steep slope. Herzog later wrote, "To everyone who reached it, Camp Five became one of the worst memories of their lives."

After a breathless, sleepless night, the two climbers left Camp Five before dawn and headed for the summit. At two o'clock on the afternoon of June 3, 1950, Herzog and his companion reached the top of Annapurna, 26,504 feet (8,078 meters) above sea level. They were standing at a spot higher than human beings had ever stood before.

After taking some photographs, the two men began their descent. Exhausted from the cold and the lack of oxygen, Herzog was no longer able to think clearly. He dropped his gloves and, as if in a dream, watched while they slid down the mountain away from him. Although he had an extra pair of socks with him to use as makeshift gloves in just such an emergency, he forgot to put them on. The two climbers hurried down the mountain to Camp Five, where two other mountaineers were waiting for them. By the time they got there, Herzog's hands and feet were frozen. The four men spent a terrible night in Camp Five.

When the climbers set out the next morning, it was snowing so hard that they couldn't find the higher of the two tents that made up Camp Four. They yelled for help, but the howling wind drowned out their cries. In danger of freezing to death, the four mountaineers huddled together in a crevasse through another long and terrifying night. By daybreak they were nearly dead. Herzog had given up all hope of rescue when he heard someone shouting; the mountaineers waiting at upper Camp Four had located them. The crevasse where Herzog and his companions had spent the night turned out to be only 200 yards (180 meters) from the upper camp.

With the aid of their friends at Camp Four, the injured climbers continued the descent. Herzog was in bad shape, his feet and hands frozen, and he could hardly keep a grip on the climbing rope. Some of the climbers had lost

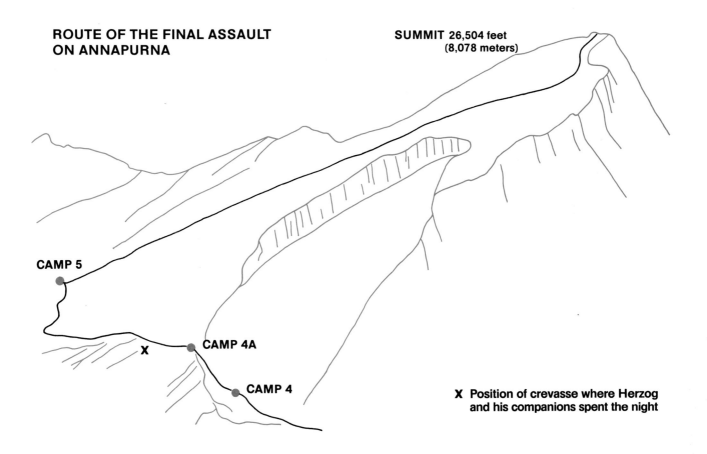

ROUTE OF THE FINAL ASSAULT ON ANNAPURNA

SUMMIT 26,504 feet
(8,078 meters)

CAMP 5

X

CAMP 4A

CAMP 4

X Position of crevasse where Herzog
and his companions spent the night

their dark goggles and couldn't open their eyes in the blinding sunlight reflecting from the ice and snow.

The descent to the base camp was sheer torture. Blinded and frozen, Herzog and some of the others had to be carried down on the backs of Sherpa porters. By the time they reached the camp, they were in danger of losing their arms and legs to frostbite. The expedition doctor saved the mens' limbs and their lives, but eventually Herzog had to have all of his fingers and toes amputated because of infections related to the frostbite.

One of the greatest mountains in the world had been conquered, but those who participated in the climb had paid a terrible price.

After the conquest of Annapurna, mountaineers set their sights on the other 8,000-meter peaks, especially Mount Everest. Rising nearly half a mile higher than Annapurna, Everest is the tallest mountain on earth. For 30 years, this frozen giant turned away all who dared approach it. Many expeditions, including one made up of 300 people, were forced to abandon their attempts before reaching the top. Some people thought Everest would never be climbed, but the success on Annapurna gave others renewed hope.

In 1953, British mountaineers launched a huge expedition made up of nearly 400 climbers, guides, and porters, all with one goal—to help someone in the team reach the top of Everest. This group had a real advantage over earlier expeditions. For the first time, the mountaineers used lightweight oxygen equipment that enabled them to breathe more easily while resting at night and while climbing.

One by one, tiny camps sprang up along the side of the giant mountain. Finally, Camp Eight clung just below the summit. After one unsuccessful try by another team, New Zealand climber Edmund Hillary and Tenzing Norgay, a Sherpa guide, set out for the top. Unable to reach it on the first day, they established Camp Nine and spent the night at an altitude of 27,900 feet (8,370 meters). On the morning of May 29, 1953, they tried once more and made it to the summit of Mount Everest, 29,028 feet (8,848 meters) above sea level. Just 16 years before astronauts reached the moon, Hillary and Norgay stood at the highest point on the surface of the earth.

Mount Everest, the world's tallest mountain. In May 1953, two climbers reached the peak of Everest, 29,028 feet (8,848 meters) above sea level.

GLOSSARY

Alpine climb—a climb similar to those common in the European Alps. An Alpine climb may include rock as well as snow or ice and can usually be done in one or two days.

anchor—a point at which a climber is firmly attached to the mountainside by means of ropes, slings, and other pieces of equipment

belayer—the person who controls the rope during a belay and is responsible for stopping another climber's fall

belaying—protecting a climber from falling by anchoring the climbing rope to some secure object

belay plate—a small metal plate used as a mechanical belaying device. The climbing rope runs through the plate rather than passing around the belayer's body.

braking hand—the hand used by a belayer or a rappeler to stop the passage of the rope and prevent a fall

carabiner—a metal ring or clip with a clasp in one side controlled by a spring. Carabiners are used in many different ways to connect pieces of climbing equipment together.

chimneys—vertical cracks or openings in a mountainside wide enough to get inside of

chock—a piece of metal that can be jammed into a small crack to provide an anchor for a belay or for some other climbing maneuver

crampons—metal frames with sharp spikes on the lower surfaces and sometimes on the tips. Attached to a climber's boots, crampons provide a secure foothold on ice and snow.

Himalayan climbs—climbs similar to those common in the Himalayas, requiring large amounts of equipment and taking many days to complete

ice ax—a special mountaineering ax that has a pointed shaft and a head with a pick on one end and a blade, or adze, on the other end

ice screws—long metal screws that can be twisted into ice to provide an anchor

jamming—establishing a hold by forcing some part of the body into a vertical crack or opening

nut—another name for a chock

pitch—one section of a climb, usually between two points where belays are established

Temple Crag in the Sierra Nevadas

pitons—metal blades with rings or eyes on one end that can be hammered into ice or cracks in rock to provide an anchor

protection—any technique or piece of equipment used to protect climbers from falling

rappeling—descending a pitch by sliding down a rope that is anchored at the top

running belay—a belay in which the rope connecting the belayer to the climber runs through one or more carabiners anchored to the slope. This kind of belay is used to protect the leader of a climbing team from a long fall.

self-arrest—a method of stopping a fall on ice or snow by digging the ice ax into the surface of the slope

sling—a loop of webbing or rope used to set up an anchor or to connect pieces of climbing equipment

The tallest mountain in Africa, snow-capped Kilimanjaro was first climbed in 1889.

MOUNTAIN CLIMBING RECORDS

MOUNTAIN	LOCATION	HEIGHT (Feet/Meters)	YEAR CLIMBED	NATIONALITY OF TEAM
Himalayan "Eight-Thousanders"				
Everest	Nepal	29,028 / 8,848	1953	British-Asian
K2	Kashmir	28,250 / 8,611	1954	Italian
Kanchenjunga	India	28,208 / 8,598	1955	British
Lhotse	Nepal	27,890 / 8,501	1956	Swiss
Makalu	Nepal	27,824 / 8,481	1955	French
Cho Oyu	Nepal	26,750 / 8,153	1954	Austrian
Dhaulagiri	Nepal	26,810 / 8,172	1960	Swiss
Nanga Parabet	Jammu-Kashmir	26,658 / 8,125	1953	German-Austrian
Manaslu	Nepal	26,650 / 8,123	1956	Japanese
Annapurna	Nepal	26,504 / 8,078	1950	French
Mountains in the United States				
McKinley	Alaska	20,320 / 6,194	1913	U.S.
Blackburn	Alaska	16,523 / 4,956	1912	U.S.
Whitney	California	14,494 / 4,418	1973	U.S.
Elbert	Colorado	14,433 / 4,399	UNKNOWN	UNKNOWN
Ranier	Washington	14,410 / 4,392	1870	U.S.
Pike's Peak	Colorado	14,110 / 4,301	1820	U.S.
Grand Teton	Wyoming	13,766 / 4,129	1898	U.S.
Other Great Mountains				
Tirich Mir	Pakistan	25,426 / 7,627	1950	Norwegian
Aconcagua	Argentina	22,831 / 6,959	1897	British
Huascaran	Peru	22,205 / 6,661	1908	U.S.*
Chimborazo	Ecuador	20,561 / 6,267	1880	British
Logan	Canada	19,520 / 5,950	1925	U.S.-Canadian
Kilimanjaro	Tanzania	19,340 / 5,895	1889	German
Citlaltepetl	Mexico	18,696 / 5,690	1848	French
Elbrus	U.S.S.R.	18,481 / 5,633	1868	British
Popocatepetl	Mexico	17,887 / 5,452	UNKNOWN	UNKNOWN
Kenya	Kenya	17,058 / 5,199	1899	British
Mount Blanc	France	15,771 / 4,807	1786	French
Matterhorn	Switzerland	14,692 / 4,478	1865	British

*This was the first great mountain to be conquered by a woman, Annie Peck.

Adapted from THE MOUNTAINS by Lorus and Margery Milne and the Editors of Time/Life, 1962.

Superwheels & Thrill Sports

Airplanes
AEROBATICS
AIRPLANE RACING
FLYING-MODEL AIRPLANES
HELICOPTERS
HOME-BUILT AIRPLANES
PERSONAL AIRPLANES
SCALE-MODEL AIRPLANES
YESTERDAY'S AIRPLANES

Automobiles & Auto Racing
AMERICAN RACE CAR DRIVERS
THE DAYTONA 500
DRAG RACING
ICE RACING
THE INDIANAPOLIS 500
INTERNATIONAL RACE CAR DRIVERS
LAND SPEED RECORD BREAKERS
RACING YESTERDAY'S CARS
RALLYING
ROAD RACING
TRACK RACING
CLASSIC SPORTS CARS
CUSTOM CARS
DINOSAUR CARS: LATE GREAT CARS
   FROM 1945 TO 1966

FABULOUS CARS OF THE 1920s & 1930s
KIT CARS: CARS YOU CAN BUILD YOURSELF
MODEL CARS
RESTORING YESTERDAY'S CARS
VANS: THE PERSONALITY VEHICLES
YESTERDAY'S CARS

Bicycles
BICYCLE ROAD RACING
BICYCLE TRACK RACING
BICYCLES ON PARADE

Motorcycles
GRAND NATIONAL CHAMPIONSHIP RACES
MOPEDS: THE GO-EVERYWHERE BIKES
MOTOCROSS MOTORCYCLE RACING
MOTORCYCLE RACING
MOTORCYCLES ON THE MOVE
THE WORLD'S BIGGEST MOTORCYCLE RACE:
   THE DAYTONA 200

Other Specialties
KARTING
MOUNTAIN CLIMBING
RIVER THRILL SPORTS
SAILBOAT RACING
SPORT DIVING
SKYDIVING
SNOWMOBILE RACING
YESTERDAY'S FIRE ENGINES
YESTERDAY'S TRAINS
YESTERDAY'S TRUCKS

Lerner Publications Company
241 First Avenue North, Minneapolis, Minnesota 55401